GOD LOVES US ALL

By REV. LAWRENCE G. LOVASIK, S.V.D.
Divine Word Missionary

NIHIL OBSTAT: Daniel V. Flynn, J.C.D., *Censor Librorum*
IMPRIMATUR: ✠ James P. Mahoney, D.D., *Vicar General,*
Archdiocese of New York

Printed in Hong Kong

CATHOLIC BOOK PUBLISHING CO.
TOTOWA, NJ

GOD MADE US

GOD made the whole world and all things. He also made us. He is our Creator.

God made us because He loves us and because He wants us to be happy with Him in heaven forever.

God made the world and us to give glory to Himself by showing us His power and goodness. He wants to share His love and happiness with us.

To gain the happiness of heaven, we must know, love and serve God in this world. We must know God if we wish to love Him. We cannot love Him unless we show it by doing what God wants us to do.

We learn to know, love and serve God from Jesus Christ, the Son of God, Who teaches us through the Catholic Church.

The Church teaches us that we serve God by keeping His commandments, by receiving the Sacraments, especially Holy Communion, by praying to God and by doing good deeds to please Him.

GOD BECAME MAN FOR US

AFTER the fall of our first parents, God promised Eve that someday one of her children would overcome Satan, who had brought sin and death into the world by tempting Eve to disobey God.

This Child Who was to come would teach man to know and love God and would bring everlasting life.

When the appointed time came God kept His promise. He sent a Redeemer into the world. This Redeemer was Jesus Christ, the greatest of all the kings, priests and prophets whom God sent to guide men.

Jesus Christ is God made man. He is God because He is the only Son of God, having the same divine nature as His Father.

He is man because He is the Son of the Blessed Virgin Mary and has a body and soul like ours. Yet Jesus is only one Person, the second Person of the Blessed Trinity.

Jesus became man and was born of the Virgin Mary so that He might suffer for us and teach us how to save our soul.

We should love Jesus Who has done so much for us to show His love.

GOD DIED FOR OUR SOUL

JESUS suffered and died on the Cross to make up for our sins and to win grace for our soul. Jesus opened heaven to us by His death on the Cross.

Before He died, Jesus told His Apostles: "There is no greater love than this: to lay down one's life for one's friends."

He also said: "I am the Good Shepherd. I know My sheep and My sheep know Me. For these sheep I will give My life."

Jesus is your Friend. He is also your Good Shepherd. He showed how much He loved you by dying on the Cross for you. He takes care of your soul, especially when you receive Him in Holy Communion and pray to Him.

Love Jesus with all your heart. Show Him how much you love Him because He gave His life for love of you and because He always remains your Friend. Show Him your love especially by going to Holy Mass because it is a remembrance of the sufferings and death of Jesus, and the sacrifice of the Cross offered to the Heavenly Father again, though in an unbloody way in this Sacrament.

JESUS HELPS US THROUGH THE SACRAMENTS

JESUS gives us His grace through the Catholic Church, which He started. The Catholic Church has Seven Sacraments through which these graces come into our soul. We must use the Sacraments to gain the grace we need to save our soul and to get to heaven.

BAPTISM gives your soul the new life of sanctifying grace by which you become a child of God and which gave you a right to heaven.

In CONFIRMATION the Holy Spirit comes to you and makes you strong in your Faith and a good Christian.

PENANCE forgives the sins you have committed since you were baptized.

The **HOLY EUCHARIST** is the Body and Blood, Soul and Divinity of Jesus Christ, under the appearances of bread and wine, offered to God in the Mass and received by you in Holy Communion.

The **ANOINTING OF THE SICK** gives health and strength to your soul, and sometimes to your body, when you are very sick or old, and may be in danger of death.

HOLY ORDERS is the Sacrament through which men receive the power and grace to be Bishops, priests and deacons.

MATRIMONY is the Sacrament that joins people in marriage and helps them to do their duties.

9

JESUS IS THE FOUNDER
OF THE CATHOLIC CHURCH

JESUS founded the Catholic Church to lead all people to heaven. He picked out twelve men, whom He called Apostles, and taught them the truths that He brought from heaven. These truths help us to save our soul because they teach us how to know and love and serve God.

Jesus also gave His Apostles the power to rule the people who belong to His Church, and to make them holy by giving them the Seven Sacraments.

Jesus made Saint Peter the head of the Apostles and of His Church. He said, "You are 'Rock' and upon this rock I will build My Church, and the jaws of death shall not overcome it. I will give you the keys of the kingdom of heaven." The Apostles were the first Bishops of His Church.

The Apostles made other Bishops by placing their hands on their foreheads and praying for God's power to be given them.

HOW JESUS TAKES CARE
OF HIS CHURCH

THE Apostles made other Bishops who would take their place when they died. All Bishops since then have the same powers that Jesus gave to the Apostles — the power to teach His truth, to forgive sins, to offer Holy Mass, and to make people holy through the Sacraments that Jesus began.

The Church, founded by Jesus Christ, began in His Death and Resurrection. It is the new People of God, guided by the Holy Spirit. It is the work of God's love for us.

In the Catholic Church are the truths of the Faith and the Sacraments. The Church carried the Good News of the Gospels to the whole world.

God wishes the Church to have leaders — the Bishops. The Church is a people guided by its Bishops, who are in union with the Pope, the Bishop of Rome, who takes the place of Jesus Christ on earth. The Pope follows Peter in the care of the flock of Christ, the Good Shepherd.

We must honor and obey our Bishops for they are our fathers and shepherds.

The priests help the Bishops to care for those who belong to the Church.

WHY JESUS FOUNDED
THE CHURCH

THE priests help the Bishops to care for those who belong to the Catholic Church. The Holy Father, Bishops, and priests take the place of Jesus in leading souls to heaven.

Jesus founded His Church *to teach us* the truths that He Himself taught, so that we might be saved and reach heaven.

Jesus founded His Church *to make us holy.* The graces that Jesus won for us on Calvary are given to us through the Sacraments. They are signs of grace that we can see, so that we may know when and what kind of grace we are receiving.

Jesus founded His Church *to rule and guide* the People of God. He wants us to know what we must do for God.

GOD SENT HIS HOLY SPIRIT
TO HIS CHURCH

GOD the Father and God the Son sent the Holy Spirit, the Third Person of the Blessed Trinity, to live in the Church.

The Holy Spirit came to the Church on the Feast of Pentecost. This is the birthday of the Church. A sound like a mighty wind filled the whole house where the Apostles had come together to pray, along with the Blessed Virgin Mary and some disciples of Jesus. Tongues of fire came down upon the head of each of them and they were filled with the Holy Spirit. Then they went out to preach to the people about Jesus Christ.

Many people accepted the message and were baptized; about three thousand became Christians on that day.

The Catholic Church cannot make a mistake in teaching people because the Holy Spirit guides it until the end of the world.

The Catholic Church is like a living body. Jesus is the Head and people are the members. The Holy Spirit is the soul of this body because He gives it life.

WHO BELONGS TO THE CHURCH?

THOSE who belong to the Catholic Church are:

1. The Saints in heaven. We must honor the Saints because they pray for us and because we honor God when we honor them.

2. The suffering souls in purgatory belong to the Church. We should pray for these souls and offer Holy Mass for them because they cannot help themselves.

3. All those on earth who believe in what the Church teaches belong to the Church.

19

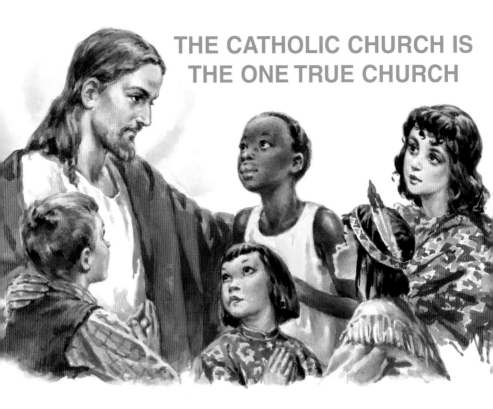

THE CATHOLIC CHURCH IS THE ONE TRUE CHURCH

THE Catholic Church is the one true Church that Jesus founded because the Catholic Church is One, Holy, Catholic and Apostolic.

The Church is ONE. This means that all Catholics all over the world believe the same things that Jesus taught. They have the same Holy Mass and Sacraments. They obey the same Holy Father, the Pope, who takes the place of Jesus on earth.

THE Catholic Church is HOLY. Jesus, Who is God Himself and all-holy, started the Catholic Church.

Its Sacraments give us grace to live a holy life. Grace gives us the life of God. It keeps us from sin and helps us to live a good life so that we may save our soul.

Grace is a help from God that gives light to our mind to know what God wants us to do to reach heaven.

THE Church is CATHOLIC, which means that it is all over the world. Jesus wanted it to help all people to get to heaven.

Before Jesus rose into heaven He said to His Apostles: "Go and make disciples of all the nations. Baptize them in the name of the Father and of the Son and of the Holy Spirit. Teach them to do everything I have commanded you."

THE Catholic Church is APOSTOLIC — this means that it is the same Church that Jesus started when He gave the Apostles His power to teach and guide all people, and to help them to be holy.

He said to the Apostles, "As the Father has sent Me, I also send you. He who hears you, hears Me."

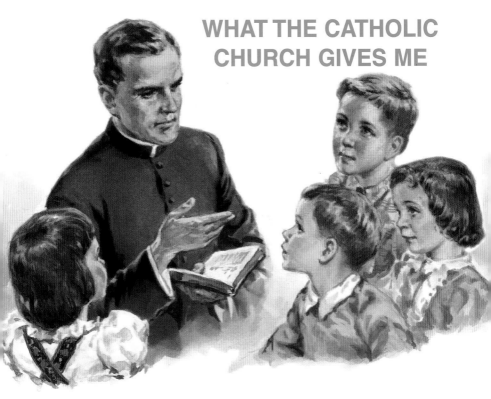

WHAT THE CATHOLIC CHURCH GIVES ME

THE Catholic Church gives me what I want most.

The Church Gives Me God's Truth

My *MIND* wants to know what is true. The Church gives me God's *truth*. This truth tells me what God has made known. It tells me what God wants me to do to reach heaven. It tells me about the Sacraments that Jesus gave us to make my soul holy by grace.

The Church Gives Me Forgiveness of Sins

M Y *SOUL* wants to be washed from its sins. The Church gives me *forgiveness of sins.* Sin is the greatest evil in the world because it displeases God and hurts our soul. It can even make us lose God forever.

In the Sacrament of Penance the priest has the power from Jesus to take away our sins when we confess them and are truly sorry for them.

The Church Gives Me God

MY *HEART* wants God. The Catholic Church gives me God. My heart needs God. He made me to know, love, and serve Him and to be happy with Him in heaven. I can never be happy without God.

The Catholic Church gives me God because through the Seven Sacraments she gives me God's grace. God lives in my soul by grace as my best Friend.

In Holy Communion God is yours most of all. The Heavenly Father gives you Jesus in the Mass as the Food of your soul. Jesus comes to visit your soul in Holy Communion. He lives in your soul and helps you to become more like Him.

The Church Gives Me a Mother

MY *HEART* also wants a mother. The Catholic Church *gives me a mother.* Jesus also gives me His own Mother as my Mother. He said from the Cross, "There is your Mother," as he spoke to St. John, who took our place at the Cross.

We can ask her for help at any time. Like our own mother, Mary is always ready to help us.

When we ask Mary for something, she places what we ask for before Jesus. We should trust our Blessed Mother in our daily prayers. She will lead us to Jesus.

THANK YOU, GOD

THANK You, God, for Your great love for me.

Thank You for letting me belong to the one true Church that Jesus gave us to lead us to heaven.

Help me to show You how much I thank You and want to love You. Help me to be a good Catholic as long as I live by obeying the Church, by using the Sacraments that she gives me to help me save my soul, and by praying often.

Thank You, God the Father my Creator, God the Son my Redeemer, God the Holy Spirit my Sanctifier, for the greatest gift You could give me—my Catholic Faith!

"I believe
in the Holy
Catholic Church."

31

GLORY be to the Father, and to the Son and to the Holy Spirit. As it was in the beginning, is now, and ever shall be world without end. Amen.